DURHAM
· The people & The place ·
1914 - 1939

A HISTORY IN PHOTOGRAPHS

By

Michael F. Richardson

with an introduction by Professor G.R. Batho

Introduction

Durham, in the words of Findley Muirhead in the <u>Blue Guide to England</u> (1919), "is probably the most romantic city in the North of England". This is almost generally agreed because of the uniqueness of the city's physical characteristics and the juxtaposition of its Romanesque Cathedral and Norman Castle on a tree-lined peninsula formed by the River Wear. This collection of photographs concentrates on Durham, the people and the place, from the outbreak of the First to that of the Second World War - on the trades of the city and the living conditions of the people, often in straitened circumstances or totally unemployed; on the public-spirited service of soldiers and civilians who fought for their country or maintained worthy traditions in sport and other leisure activities; and on ways in which people enjoyed such spare time and such meagre opportunities for festivity as they had. Some 816 men of the 8th Battalion of the Durham Light Infantry perished in the First World War, many of them from the city. More happily, the County was acknowledged at the time as the leading area for amateur dramatics in the country.

But all was not beautiful in the city which Arthur Mee declared in 1953 "one of the brighter jewels in the English diadem of beauty" (<u>The King's England</u>). The Medical Officer of Health's Report for 1919 records a sorry number of infectious diseases. Only 16 deaths were attributed to influenza despite the famous epidemic in the early part of the year, though this was in all probability an underestimation and no fewer than 116 cases of measles, 56 of scarlet fever, and 33 of tuberculosis were reported. 42 deaths occurred from bronchitis, 23 from pneumonia, 24 from tuberculosis and 3 from diphtheria. In 1928 the Bishop (Hensley Henson) had to lead a national appeal for the urgent restoration of the Castle and the strengthening of its foundations which were literally shifting. At the same time unemployment in the region was rife, especially as the two industries on which the North East principally relied, shipbuilding and mining, had lost much of their overseas markets.

Joan Conquest the novelist, herself an ex-nurse, came to Durham in September 1933 and declared the slums, particularly those of Milburngate and Framwellgate, the worst in the country: "The abominable dirty, sunless yards - breeding grounds for disease - and the appalling state of the tenements are a positive disgrace to a civilised country" (Durham Advertiser). The Council pursued an active slum-clearing policy, but by 1944 when Thomas Sharp put forward his development plan for the City (Cathedral City, The Architectural Press) he could write of Durham's "share of mean and squalid 19th-century housing", of its "filthied" river "black as ink" with "the consistency of treacle", and of its "air of grimness and neglect" which rendered North Road, the principal shopping street, reminiscent "of a mining town rather than a cathedral city", though only a fifth of Durham's insured population worked in the coal industry in the period. At the end of the Second World War, Durham remained sadly deficient for public facilities like an art gallery and a theatre, and the existence of cinemas and of a popular ice-rink was not enough to create a centre of culture.

The General Strike of 1926 and the Jarrow March of 1936 highlighted the plight of the working people in Britain between the Wars and especially in the Durham area. Because of the extensive public assistance which had to be provided, the rates charge in Durham was 8s. 6d., against an average of 2s. 8½d., in 1934. Yet there is plenty of testimony to the buoyant spirit of the local people, to their grit and to their determination to win through. Mrs.

Edna Scott, a miner's daughter from Crook born in 1928, in her poem "Memories" records :

> The rooms were draughty, dark and damp.
> The house was old with creaks on every stair.
> The plaster crumbled, moist and grey,
> The bathroom was a dream away,
> But we were happy there.

Mrs. Joyce Ord, another miner's daughter from Elisabethville, Birtley, born in 1927, in a letter to me this year remarked :

> Those were happy days when everyone chipped in and helped each other, and
> could go out even all day, and not lock your doors and windows.

There was very little money but children rarely went hungry and generally felt loved And out of 339 births in a population of 16,746 in the City in 1919, only 20 were illegitimate.

Are there lessons to be learned from the history of the region between the Wars? We must not see the "Good Old Days" through rose coloured spectacles, nor fail to remember the ability to overcome adversity. Mr. Richardson's photographs remind us of an eventful era in the evolution of the City and will stimulate memories, both glad and sad, for many who lived in the region during the period.

Professor G. R. Batho

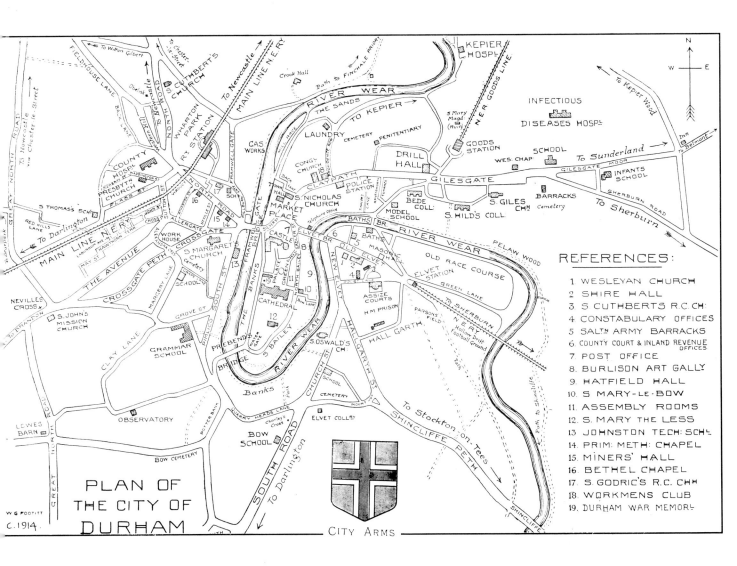

PLAN OF THE CITY OF DURHAM

W G FOOTITT

C. 1914.

CITY ARMS

REFERENCES:

1. WESLEYAN CHURCH
2. SHIRE HALL
3. S CUTHBERTS R.C. CH:
4. CONSTABULARY OFFICES
5. SALTN ARMY BARRACKS
6. COUNTY COURT & INLAND REVENUE OFFICES
7. POST OFFICE
8. BURLISON ART GALLY
9. HATFIELD HALL
10. S MARY-LE-BOW
11. ASSEMBLY ROOMS
12. S. MARY THE LESS
13. JOHNSTON TECH: SCHL
14. PRIM: METH: CHAPEL
15. MINERS' HALL
16. BETHEL CHAPEL
17. S. GODRIC'S R.C. CHM
18. WORKMENS CLUB
19. DURHAM WAR MEMORL

Durham Railway Station, Southbound platform, 3 September 1914. Recruits for Kitchener's New Army leaving for Richmond, Yorkshire, to join the Green Howards. Most of these men were recruited from the Framwellgate and Sidegate area of the City. The feeling throughout the country was that it would be all over by Christmas. It is likely that half the men in this picture did not return home.

The premises of William Wasey, Saddler and Harness Maker, 28 Claypath, c.1915. The site was later occupied by the Palladium Cinema.

The Count's House, c.1915. This area was known as Count's Corner because of Count Boruwlaski (1739-1837), the famed Polish dwarf. He lodged at the home of the Ebdon family for the last years of his life. They lived in a large house near the site of the present 'Count's House'. The building was a summer house belonging to a house in the South Bailey. You can see from the photograph that it was a popular place to call and have tea and scones.

Durham City Horse Parade entrant at the Barracks, c.1915. The factory of Quakers Sauce Co., drysalters, stood at Ellis Leazes, Gilesgate. To the left Mr. Lockerbie, a blacksmith from Gilesgate, and to the right Mr. Fred Elliott, a driver with the company.

Pte. Albert Richardson, 8th D.L.I., 1915, son of Albert Richardson, Head Gardener at St.Hild's College, Gilesgate. Young Albert was a bugler and served in France during the Great War. Albert Jnr. also became Head Gardener at St. Hild's.

2nd Lieut. Geraint Pasco Francis Thomas, 2nd D.L.I., c.1915. Son of the Rev. F. Thomas, Vicar of St. Giles', Durham, he was attached to the Royal Flying Corps and was shot down over France in 1916. He spent the remainder of the war as a prisoner. (See p.22 for a photograph of his father.)

An interesting cart belonging to McNaughton's Steam Laundry, 15 Claypath c.1915. The laundry picked up and delivered customers' washing and cleaning. It was obviously a service for those who could afford it.

The Market Place, Durham. Presentations to local heroes, June 1917. Pte. Richard Savage, 10th Royal Hussars (awarded D.C.M. in October 1914), Sgt. W. H. Smith, M.M., D.L.I., Pte. M. Hanley, M.M., D.L.I. The Mayor in the centre is Frank W. Goodyear and at the back on the far right is the Very Revd. Herbert Hensley Henson, at that time Dean of Durham, later Bishop (1920-39).

A 34 seater A.E.C. bus bought by the United Bus Company c.1918. This bus is seen here at the top of Millburngate. Above the rear of the bus can be seen the shop sign of J. G. Rollin Limited, Chemist, 3 South Street (see page 23 for photograph of Rollin's shop.)

John Davies, Bugler in St.Margaret's Church Lads' Brigade, Crossgate, c.1918. Uniformed youth organisations were popular at the time. St. Margaret's Church Lads' Brigade continued until 1983.

An illuminated address, given to all who served their country in the Great War, from the Mayor, Aldermen and Citizens of Durham and Framwellgate, July 1919.

A performance of Aladdin (" A lad in and out ") at St. Margaret's Church Hall, Durham, c.1920. Amateur operatics have a long tradition in the North East.

Coach and Four, used for transporting the Assize Judges from Durham Castle to the Assize Court, c.1920 (the Assize Court was abolished in 1971). The coach is standing at Elvet Waterside, behind the present day County Hotel. This narrow road led up to Elvet Bridge. To the right of the photograph you can see the spire of St. Nicholas' Church.

St. Nicholas' Church Bell Ringing Team 1920. Top row : P. Hodgson, A. Robinson, C. Pattison, T. Brownless. Bottom row : H. Pattison, E. Allison, J. Henderson (Bell Major), W. McIntyre, S. Burdon. The bells are no longer used.

The Norman Church of St.Giles c.1920. The headstones were removed in the early 1960s. Most of the headstones were destroyed; a small number were kept and stand against the churchyard wall. A new vicarage now stands to the right of the picture.

The Rev. Francis Thomas, September 1921, Vicar of St. Giles' Church and Chaplain to St. Mary's Home (The County Penitentiary) 1901-1921. The Penitentiary is now University accommodation for overseas students! The Rev. Thomas is buried in the 1870 churchyard of St. Giles'; a fine granite cross marks his last resting place. (See p.12 for a photograph of his son.)

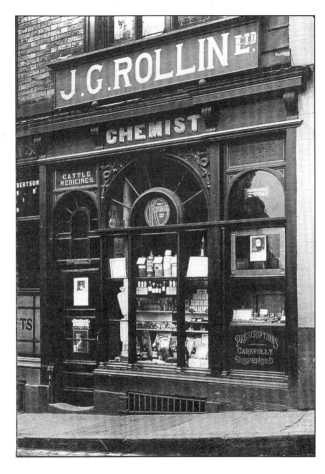

An attractive shop front of J. G. Rollin Limited, Chemist, 3 South Street, Durham, c.1921. This building stood below the Fighting Cocks Public House.

An interesting publicity photograph advertising William Stones, Window Cleaner, 26 Claypath, Durham, c.1920. The property is the 1906 extension to the Johnston School, South Street. The School was named after the famous James Finlay Weir Johnston, Reader in Chemistry at Durham University, who died in 1855.

Mr. William Nicholls behind the steering wheel of a steam roller. This shot was taken near the Green in Gilesgate in 1923. Mr. Nicholls came up from Norfolk especially to work on this contract. Later he married a girl from Carrville and after travelling throughout the country working with steam, he settled in Durham City in 1941.

New road surfaces being laid at the bottom of Gilesgate Bank, 1923. The buildings to the right and left were demolished for the new Leazes roundabout in the early 1960s.

Old Durham Gardens, 1924. The Gardens were an attractive layout of flower beds, ornamental statues and a bandstand. The garden was attached to the Pineapple Inn and dances were held there up to the 1940s. The Inn had lost its licence in 1926 owing to its then unfavourable reputation, and only sold soft drinks thereafter. The Inn is now a private house.

The old rope bridge which crossed the Wear between Kepier Wood and Brasside, c.1925. This bridge was used by miners to cross the river when working at different drifts. In the dry season the concrete blocks which supported the bridge can be seen in the river.

The Battery at Wharton Park, showing the guns, c.1925. The battery was built for a local Militia group for training and drilling exercises. The guns were taken away at the start of the 2nd World War to be melted down for the war effort.

Durham City Horse Parade entrant. The decorated cart of Wood & Watson's, 132 Gilesgate, c.1925, Durham's longest surviving Mineral Water Manufacturers, established in 1890. In 1932 they were awarded a prize medal and diploma at the Brewers Exhibition for their Stone Ginger Beer. This shot was taken near the Methodist Chapel opposite the Green. It is interesting to note the Joy Makers of the World, Keystone Cop, Charlie Chaplin and Buster Keaton.

Mr. John Metcalfe outside his workshop, 106 Gilesgate, c.1925. John, a cartwright and undertaker, traded under his uncle's name Blenkinsop. The premises are now occupied by the Dunelm Veterinary Group. The cart in the foreground was in for repair from Dimambro's Ice Cream. The gentleman to the right was evidently a debt collector.

Durham City Gipsy Juveniles, c.1926. This photograph was taken near the Horse-Hole in Millburngate. The building in the background was part of Blagdon's Leather Works.

A back street view in Claypath, c.1926. This is typical of the overcrowded conditions in the City at the time. These properties stood below the Travellers Rest Public House. At one time this was the main entrance to St. Nicholas' Vicarage, and also the entrance to the Quaker burial ground (which still exists). The buildings in the photograph were believed to have dated from the seventeenth century.

An interesting inside view of the Wearmouth Bridge Hotel, which stood at 17 Claypath, c.1927. The landlord was a Mr. Suggett.

Durham City Horse Parade Entrant in 1927. The buildings in the background are Wood & Watson's, Gilesgate, and the old gatehouse for the Militia Barracks. The cart is from the Durham Co-operative Society, 6 Claypath, and was painted by Harrison's Coach Builders, Sunderland Road. The Durham Co-operative Society was inaugurated in a very humble way by 29 men employed by Henderson's Carpet Factors. Together they raised the sum of £28; with this they purchased a chest of tea and other small items and commenced business in June 1861. The shop was a small room in Gilesgate.

Durham City Horse Parade entrant. A cart from Fowler's the grocers, 100 Claypath, c.1927. Fowler's were established in the 1850s. The man holding the horse is Jack Pickering from Palace Lane and the young lad dressed as a clown is Tom Pattison. The building in the background is part of the old gatehouse belonging to the Barracks. This area is now a car park for Wood & Watson's.

The County War Memorial, which is situated under the Rose Window of Durham Cathedral. This rare photograph captures the unveiling as the curtain falls. The time is 12 noon Saturday 24 November 1928. To the left of the memorial is the Lord Lieutenant, the Marquess of Londonderry. Mr. H. Tyson of Liverpool executed the sculpture of the stone work to the designs by Professor C. H. (later Sir Charles) Reilly of Liverpool University. The memorial was erected by Messrs. Frank W. Goodyear & Son from Gilesgate. The ceremony was attended by representatives from the Army, Navy and Airforce.

The Northumberland Hussars, B. Squadron, Football Team 1928. The headquarters for B. Squadron was the Barracks, Gilesgate (Vane Tempest Hall). Ambrose Savage is in the second row on the far right. Most of the men here were from the Durham City area, as B. Squadron were territorials.

Edward, Prince of Wales (later Edward VIII), inspecting members of the British Legion in Durham Market Place, May 1929. The Prince later went on to inspect restoration work at Durham Castle.

The West End Football Team from Framwellgate, c.1930. Two of the Team were spotted by a scout and became professional players. Top row : (unknown), Jackie Clough, (unknown), 2nd row : Tommy Whitfield, (unknown), Billy Hutchinson, Ernie Mcleod, Ralph Pedwell, front row : Tommy Robson, Tony Robson (mascots).

Old Beaver, one of Durham's lost characters, seen here standing outside Carroll's lodging house which stood near the Horse-Hole in Millburngate, c.1929 Old Beaver, as he was known, was a permanent lodger at Mrs. Carroll's. The young boy is Jack Adamson, Mrs. Carroll's grandson.

Coal mine workings at Kepier Wood, c.1930. This track was operated by cable. The wheel on the right of the photograph was used to guide the wire cable which pulled the coaltubs. Evidence of Coal Drifts can still be seen in the wood.

Little Hazel Davies sitting on the Blue Stone in St. Giles' Churchyard, 1932. The Blue Stone is thought to have been a meteorite. Originally it stood at the bottom of Gilesgate Bank next to the Dry Bridge. Its origins are a mystery. In 1923 it was taken to the churchyard for safe keeping when the Dry Bridge was removed. It became a local curiosity for many years, having a shiny blue look caused by children sliding over the surface. It disappeared from the churchyard in the 1960s when nearby council houses were built. The photograph was taken by Hazel's uncle, Foster Davies, who was churchwarden at St. Giles'.

Elvet railway bridge, c.1933. This bridge stood near Hollow Drift which is near Maiden Castle. Elvet North Eastern Railway Station is where the present Magistrates' Courts stand. In the centre of the photograph can be seen the old Gazebo at Old Durham Gardens.

The old Woolpack, 11 Framwellgate. This photograph was taken on Saturday 18 March 1933, the day after Denham Ringwood was murdered by his wife in the upstairs room above the policeman. The Woolpack was a tenement property with several families living in the same building.

A very interesting view showing the Vane Tempest Hall, Gilesgate, c.1933, the last surviving example of a Militia Barracks in County Durham, built in 1865. In 1884 the Barracks were taken over as a smallpox hospital for the city. This view shows the allotments below the old cemetery. The whole area of the allotments had been one of the ash tips for the city from the 1880s to the 1920s.

Ploughing near Old Durham Gardens c.1933. The hill on the right is known as Maiden Castle. It is believed to have been of late prehistoric origin possibly Bronze Age or Iron Age. An archaeological dig was carried out here in 1956.

A street party to celebrate the Silver Jubilee of King George V and Queen Mary in 1935 at Magdalene Street, named after the medieval hospital of St. Mary Magdalene, the ruined chapel of which can be seen just off the Gilesgate roundabout.

Children from Hilda Avenue and Oswald Avenue, Sherburn Road Estate, sitting down to a Coronation tea organised by Mrs. Gray, Deputy Mayoress, seen to the right holding a Coronation mug, May 1937. Her daughter Miss Gray is standing to the left in the light overcoat.

Fillingham's, Elvet Bridge, c.1938, Durham's oldest surviving photographers. A first class service has been given to the people of Durham by this business for most of this century.

A charming view looking down Crossgate, c.1938. St. Margaret's Church, c.1150, can be seen to the right. The presence of the sheep is a reminder of the rural nature of the City at the time.

A charming view of the City from Mountjoy Hill overlooking the Parish of St. Oswald's. The young lad in the foreground is harrowing the land, 1938.

King George VI and Queen Elizabeth visiting the new housing estate at Sherburn Road, Gilesgate, February 1939. Here the Royal Party are seen leaving the home of Mr. & Mrs. Albrighton at Fir Avenue. The Mayor is Wilfred Edge, a native of Cardiff, who came to Durham to work as a miner. At his sixth attempt he succeeded in gaining a seat on the Durham City Council, representing Framwellgate Ward. He became Durham's first Labour Mayor.

Children from Bluecoat School, Claypath, 1939, on a gas-alert drill in the schoolyard at the outbreak of the Second World War. Gas masks had to be carried at all times.

MAYORS OF DURHAM 1914 - 1939

Year	Date	Name	Year	Date	Name
1914	09 November	Peter James Waite, M.A., J.P.	1928	09 November	Walter William Wilkinson
1915	09 November	John George Gradon	1929	09 November	Henry Murdoch
1916	09 November	Frank William Goodyear	1930	10 November	John William Pattinson
1917	09 November	Arthur Pattison	1931	09 November	Joseph Watson Wood
1918	09 November	George Henderson Proctor	1932	09 November	Christopher Wilkinson
1919	10 November	William Henry Wood	1933	09 November	James Chisman Fowler
1920	10 November	William Thwaites	1934	09 November	Thomas Plummer
1921	09 November	William Smith	1935	09 November	William Robert Henry Gray
1922	09 November	Robert McLean, J.P.	1936	09 November	Charles Stewart Henry Vane-Tempest Stewart, 7th Marquess of Londonderry, K.G.
1923	09 November	Edwin Laidler			
1924	10 November	Thomas William Holiday	1937	09 November	William Ewart Bradley
1925	09 November	Peter James Waite, M.A., J.P.	1938	09 November	Wilfred Francis Edge
1926	09 November	Frank William Goodyear	1939	09 November	Sydney Kipling

Acknowledgements

Thanks are due to all those who have helped, including:
Mr. Roger Norris, Durham University Library; the staff at Durham City Reference Library; Durham Arts, Libraries & Museums Department, Durham County Council; Mrs. M. Davies, Mr . Ray Kitching, Mr. George Lye, Mrs. L. Middleton, Mr. Mark McNamara, Mr. George Nichols, Mr. Milbourne, Mr. Jim Patton, Mr. J. Pickering, the late Mrs. Doreen Plumb, Mrs. Norma Richardson, Mr. J. Robinson, Miss. F. Thomas, Mrs. Wasey, Mrs. H. Webster, Mr. Trevor Woods Durham University Archaeology Department., The map on page 5 is based on one drawn by the late W.G. Footitt.